Bar Barakah

A Parent's Guide to a Christian Bar Mitzvah

by
Craig Hill

FAMILY FOUNDATIONS INTERNATIONAL
P.O. Box 320
Littleton, CO 80160

Family Foundations International
P.O. Box 320
Littleton, Colorado 80160
Printed in the United States of America

All scripture quotations, not otherwise noted, appear in The New King
James Bible. The following versions have also been used: The New American Standard Bible, The Lockman Foundation, 1960, 1962, 1963, 1968,
1971, 1973, 1975; King James Version, Thomas Nelson, Inc., Publishers;
The Amplified Bible, Zondervan Bible Publishers, 1965, 12th Printing,
1975, The New King James Bible, Broadman & Holman Publishers, 1988.

First Printing: 1998

CONTENTS

Introduction
BLESSING OR CURSING

"When Esau heard the words of his father, he cried with an exceedingly great and bitter cry, and said to his father, 'Bless me—me also, O my father!' But he said, 'Your brother came with deceit and has taken away your blessing.' And Esau said, 'Is he not rightly named Jacob? For he has supplanted me these two times. He took away my birthright, and now look, he has taken away my blessing!' And he said, 'Have you not reserved a blessing for me?' So Esau hated Jacob because of the blessing with which his father blessed him, and Esau said in his heart, 'The days of mourning for my father are at hand; then I will kill my brother Jacob.'" **Genesis 27:34-36;41**

There is something on the inside of every person that longs for blessing from parents. In the above biblical account of Jacob and Esau, Esau deeply understood and longed for the blessing of the firstborn son from his father. When he realized that this was stolen from him by his brother Jacob, he cried out to his father with a loud wail. In the end, he was so embittered against his brother that he vowed to kill him.

In modern times we have not understood the significance and power of a parental blessing. Both Jacob and Esau knew the power of their father's blessing. It was something so powerful that Jacob and his mother

1

were willing to lie and deceive his father to get it. In the context of our Family Foundations Basic Seminar, we talk about seven critical times in which a person was meant to receive a blessing in a significant way. In this book, we will focus upon one of these critical times, the time of puberty.

Let us first start out with the meaning of the Hebrew word "to bless." This is the word **baruch**. *Baruch* literally means to kneel down before someone. However, one of the primary spiritual connotations of this word is **to empower to prosper**. Thus, to bless someone is to empower that person to prosper. When a father blesses his son or daughter, he literally empowers him/her to prosper. When I use the word prosper, I am not just re-ferring to the realm of finances. I simply mean to thrive, to do well, to succeed. So, to empower one to prosper means to set the stage for that person to do well, thrive and succeed in many areas of life, including marriage, with children, in finances, in health, in career, in minis-try, etc.

In following the lineage of Esau down through several generations, it was evident that they did not pros-per. They were the Edomites, who were never a great kingdom and were frequently overrun by enemies. The descendants of Jacob, the Israelites, on the other hand, mightily prospered. They became a great nation and pros-pered in many ways. This same principle holds true for modern families. Those children whose parents have blessed them tend to prosper for many generations, while, on the other hand, those families whose parents actively cursed them or at least did not bless them tend not to prosper for many generations.

When we are talking about blessing and cursing, we are not talking about flattery and profanity. We are rather talking about God's impartation and Satan's impartation of identity and destiny in peoples' lives. Identity is simply the answer to the question, "Who am I? Who is this 'me' that I must live with each day?" Destiny is the answer to the question, "Why am I here? What is my purpose?" Either God or Satan can answer these questions in each of our hearts. However, neither God nor Satan tends to impart messages of identity or destiny directly, but rather operates through human agency. As a matter of fact, God was so concerned that each of us receive His impartation rather than the devil's that He placed His agents in each of our lives to ensure that this would happen. **These agents are called parents.** If parents do nothing else on this earth regarding their children, the one thing God intended for them to do is to make sure that they are agents of God's impartation of identity and destiny to their children and not agents of Satan's impartation. Thus, blessing is God's mechanism of imparting identity and destiny, and cursing is the devil's mechanism of imparting identity and destiny. For more detailed explanation of this, see my book, *The Ancient Paths*.

Blessing is God's mechanism of settling identity and destiny in the heart. Without it, many people spend a lifetime trying to settle in their own way the internal issues of identity and destiny. (Am I of any value? Do I belong? Do I have a purpose?) I believe that God intended for these questions to be answered and the heart to be set at rest through a parental blessing meant to come at the time of puberty. This was intended by God to happen for every person ever born on planet Earth. It is interesting to note that virtually every culture on Earth has some sort of a rite of passage from childhood into adulthood, except our western European culture. I don't believe that this is an accident. God put these traditions, ceremonies and rites of passage into every culture of the world. In some cultures, the devil has perverted the tradition, but in our culture, he has totally eradicated nearly any trace of God's original intent.

Chapter 1
BLESSING IS AN ANCIENT PATH

Some people have thought that a rite of passage from childhood into adulthood was no longer necessary in our modern culture and that to practice such was primitive or old-fashioned. I don't believe that the parental blessing releasing a child into adulthood at the time of puberty is old-fashioned. It's **Ancient**.

"Thus says the Lord, 'Stand by the ways and see and ask for the ancient paths, Where the good way is, and walk in it; And you shall find rest for your souls. But they said, 'We will not walk in it.'" Jeremiah 6:16 (NASB)

When I first ran across this verse years ago, the phrase **ancient paths** jumped off the page at me. When I looked up the meaning of the Hebrew word "ancient," I found that it did not just mean old or old-fashioned. It was the Hebrew word "OLAM" for which I found many meanings such as hidden, concealed, universal, perpetual, timeless, universal, eternal, out of eternity. These meanings really grabbed my heart as I came to understand that God was speaking here of returning to ways that were not just old ways of men, but rather were the eternal ways of God. I believe that these OLAM/ancient ways are universal life principles, not just applicable to the Jewish culture, or any specific culture, but rather applicable to all mankind.

The ancient paths are ways of God that simply cause life to work. When God created man on the Earth, He infused in man His ancient paths. It is interesting to note that even after sin entered the world, men used to live 900 years. I don't believe that this was only because the firmament was still in place and the cosmic radiation had not yet hit man. I believe that it was because men still walked, to a great degree, in the ancient paths of God. The farther we have come along in history, the farther we have departed from the ancient paths. Now when someone talks about returning to the ancient paths, most people have no clue what the ancient paths of God might entail.

The focus of this book is on one ancient path: parental blessing of children at the time of puberty to release them into adulthood. This is not a Jewish tradition, nor a primitive ceremony. It is an Ancient Path. This is something that God intended for every person to experience. Jeremiah 6:16 tells us that when we walk in the ancient paths, we will find rest for our souls. I notice that most people today, even believers in Jesus, are not at rest regarding identity and destiny. Many people spend a lifetime trying to become "valuable," because on the inside they do not feel valuable. They are trying to "become a success" by earning enough money, attaining a high enough position, doing some great work for God, or being supermom, etc. I talk to believers all the time who are 30, 40 and even 50 years old who are still trying to figure out what they want to do when they grow up.

This is <u>not normal</u>. It is very common, but it is not normal. This is not what God intended for life to be like. Such experience is a result of departing from God's ancient paths.

Life experience has not always been like this. I was shocked a few years ago when I heard a lecture on United States history given by David Barton. I had realized that it must have taken tremendous courage and character for the American colonists to stand up against the most powerful empire in the world, Great Britain, and found a new nation. I understood that there must have been a great sense of destiny and calling to do so. In order to possess the courage, character, and settled sense of identity and destiny that it took to found a new nation, I naturally assumed that most of these people were seasoned veterans of life, at least in their fifties and sixties. I was shocked to find out that several of the people who are household names to us in the US were young adults in their teens or early twenties when they said and did the things for which they are now famous.

I was astounded to discover that John Quincy Adams was sent overseas as deputy ambassador from the newly founded nation of the United States of America to the nation of Russia at age fourteen. How many fourteen-year-olds do you know today whom you would be willing to send overseas as an ambassador from your nation? If you ask your average fourteen-year-old today about the purpose and destiny of his/her life, you will probably hear about Nintendo, TV, "have fun" or other such "powerful," long term goals. Two hundred years ago, people commonly practiced law and medicine, started businesses and got married at age sixteen, seventeen and eighteen.

Here is a scary thought. How many thirty-year-olds do you know whom you would be willing to send overseas as an ambassador from your nation? In many cases, we are not seeing in thirty-year-olds today the identity, destiny and character that was in fourteen-year-olds two hundred years ago. Why not? We have departed from the ancient paths. Two hundred years ago, parents prepared their children to fulfill a destiny, not to have a job. Today, many people are wanderers on the planet simply trying to pay their bills, keep their marriages and families from disaster and survive until the end of life. There is an endless search for significance and purpose, but a continual restlessness and nagging question, "Am I really loved or valuable? Am I doing anything that has any true significance or meaning?"

How were these deep questions of the soul meant to be answered? I believe that God intended these issues to be settled right at the time of puberty through a powerful impartation of identity and destiny from God coming through a father. In cultures where this is still practiced, there is very little gender confusion in adulthood. Most people experience a strong sense of belonging, value, significance and destiny.

I remember a Jewish friend of mine, Jeff Brodsky, telling me that even as much as he loves his wife and as special as his wedding day was, there is one day that stands out more in his mind than even his wedding day.

That was the day of his Bar Mitzvah ceremony. Jeff told me that it was the most important day of his life. He said, "I can remember at what moment I woke up, because I looked at the clock. I remember what I ate for breakfast that day, the clothes I wore to the synagogue, and what people said to me. It was the day I became a man." Again, this is not a Jewish tradition, but rather is "OLAM," an ancient path meant for every son and daughter. Over the last hundred years or so, Satan has stolen this ancient path right out of our culture to the degree that it virtually never happens for anyone any more.

In the Jewish culture, a son or daughter experiencing this ceremony of blessing into adulthood is traditionally called a "Bar Mitzvah" ("Son of the Law" in Hebrew), or "Bat Mitzvah" ("Daughter of the Law.") Many people have thought that Bar Mitzvah was the name of the ceremony, but it actually pertains specifically to the person. I would like to suggest that as believers in Yeshua (Jesus) the Messiah, we would call our children passing through such a ceremony a "**Bar Barakáh**," (bar ber-aw-káw) or "**Bat Barakáh**," (bot ber-aw-káw) which is in Hebrew a "**Son of the Blessing**," or "**Daughter of the Blessing**."

Bar Barakah

Chapter 2
WHAT DOES BLESSING DO?

As we mentioned earlier, one of the primary connotations of the Hebrew word *Baruch*, to bless, is to empower to prosper. Thus, blessing at the time of puberty empowers a son or daughter to prosper in his/her adult life. If you can remember back to the time of puberty, it was sort of a fearful time. There is so much change going on in your mind, emotions and physical body. Usually, for the first time you must undress before your peers in the school locker room for P. E. class. Everyone is checking each other out, and everyone is fearful that there is something wrong with him/her. Sure enough, the devil will always see to it that there is someone there to confirm your fears and let you know that you are in some way inadequate as a man or a woman. It was God's intent to settle male and female adult identity through a ceremonial blessing from a father. When this truly happens, no one else can shake or discredit your manhood or womanhood.

Ceremonial blessing at the time of puberty releases a son or daughter spiritually and emotionally into manhood or womanhood. It establishes a settled sense of identity and destiny in the soul. The reason I say "ceremonial blessing" is because the ceremony is very important. In our modern culture that value of ceremony has all but disappeared. Ceremonies bring emotional closure to certain seasons of life and issue in new seasons. Without ceremony, many times there is no emotional closure in the heart of the person. A man still feels like a boy inside, or a woman like a girl. Let me illustrate the point utilizing the marriage ceremony, which most people understand.

I have had the following conversation with many married couples. "Are you married?," I ask. "Yes," they answer. "Are you certain you're married?" Looking at each other and giggling, they both answer, "Yes, I'm certain we're married." I then continue, "How do you know you're married?" "I just know I am," they reply. "When did you become married?," I ask. They will then respond with the date of their wedding. "After you had your wedding, did you immediately the next day begin introducing this woman as your wife, or this man as your husband?" "Yes, immediately the next day." "Has there ever been a time since your wedding when you woke up in the morning and thought, 'I wonder if I'm really married. Maybe it didn't take. Maybe we should redo the ceremony.'" Again they look at each other, laugh and say, "No, I've always since my wedding day known I was married." I then say, "Now you may have had days when you wished you weren't married, but you're telling me that there has never been one day when you questioned whether you were really married or not?" They answer, "That's right. Not one day."

Now, what gives a couple such assuredness and internal confidence that they are married? It is the wedding ceremony. I have not gotten the same type of confident, "You've got to be kidding; what a stupid question" type of answers from unmarried people simply living together. The wedding ceremony brings an emotional closure to single life and an absolute internal assurance that one is now married. This was God's intention. Again, marriage and the wedding ceremony are not old or old-fashioned traditions. A wedding is OLAM, an ancient path of God.

In the same way that a wedding ceremony brings emotional closure to single life and a release and internal confidence regarding the fact that one is married, so the ceremonial blessing at puberty brings emotional closure to childhood and a release and confidence regarding one's own manhood or womanhood. Once this has happened, no one can steal your identity and destiny from you. A man who knows he is a man does not have to prove his manhood to himself or anyone else. When spiritual and emotional closure has been brought to the issue, it doesn't matter what anyone else says or does. Manhood or womanhood is not at stake in the ridicule or rejection of others. It is settled. This brings the soul into peace.

When there has not been a proper release into manhood or womanhood through ceremonial blessing by parents, there oftentimes remains in the heart a lingering feeling of childhood. This feeling is not logical and does not go away with age. I have spoken with many grown people who tell me that on the inside they still feel like little boys or little girls. Some keep waiting for a certain age for the feeling to go away.

However, this feeling is not age-dependent. Some think, "Well, when I'm 21, then I'll be a man." Twenty-one comes and goes, but the feeling of being just a little boy remains. He then thinks, "Well, maybe at thirty." Thirty comes and goes, but the feeling remains. He then thinks, "Forty will be the big change." However, the feeling of childhood does not go away at 30, 40 50 or even 60. I was speaking this in one meeting and a gentleman in the front row piped up, "Brother, it doesn't go away at eighty-three." That was his age, and he could relate to the feeling of being a dumb little kid even at age eighty-three.

The feeling of not really being an adult is not dependent on age, but rather dependent upon an emotional release into adulthood. This is why God intended for everyone to experience a powerful release into adulthood through the ceremonial blessing of a father at the time of puberty. When this takes place, this blessing in a healthy and right way severs identity from the mother and releases the son or daughter into adulthood. Without it, the identity oftentimes remains tied to the mother, and the person is retained in emotional childhood.

Another consequence of not being released into adulthood at the time of puberty is a continual striving to prove manhood or womanhood. I believe that this is the root of much of the sexual immorality currently rampant among young people. A young woman who has never been blessed and released by her father may go in search of acceptance through provocatively dressing or attempting to attract the sexual attention of young men. A young man who is not settled in his own identity as a man will frequently strive to become a man through the sexual conquest of women. These, of course, are not the actions of a man, but rather those of an insecure little boy living inside a man's body. A true man or woman is secure in himself/herself and has no need to prove his/her manhood/womanhood to himself/herself or anyone else. It is a settled issue.

If young people are not released into adulthood through the ceremonial blessing of parents, many times they will strive to release themselves into adulthood. The devil is only too happy to oblige them with many counterfeits. Many join gangs in search of a counterfeit family and a counterfeit release into adulthood. Gangs have ways to become a man or a woman. Kill a rival gang member or some other such "heroic" deed and one can be deemed a man or woman in a gang. Others are compelled to attempt some daring feat to prove their adulthood. Others leave home and join the military, usually the Marine Corps. Others become ensnared in homosexuality in search of the blessing and affirmation that should have come from a father and never did. Others simply spend a lifetime striving after "success," always coming up short, and still frequently feeling like a foolish little boy or girl inside.

HOW IMPORTANT IS BLESSING?

It is interesting to note that the blessing of the father is so important that Jesus the Messiah did not perform one miracle or preach one message until after the blessing of God His Father was pronounced upon him.

In the gospel of Luke, Chapter 3 we read:

"And the Holy Spirit descended in bodily form like a dove upon Him, and a voice came from heaven which said, 'You are My beloved Son; in You I am well pleased.'" Luke 3:22

When we read the above phrase spoken by the Father over Jesus, it is unfamiliar to most of us. I am told that it was not an unfamiliar phrase to the Jews of that time. They all would have heard this phrase, "This is my beloved son in whom I am well pleased" many times. I am told that this was a common phrase spoken by every Jewish father over his son at the son's Bar Mitzvah. Thus, anyone who had ever attended a Bar Mitzvah ceremony would be familiar with this phrase.

The only person over whom this phrase could not be spoken was a person of illegitimate or questionable birth. Because of the strange manner in which Jesus' birth occurred, it was not understood and was thus considered illegitimate by most. Furthermore, since Jesus was not Joseph's biological son, he probably did not pronounce this blessing over Jesus at the time of his Bar Mitzvah ceremony.

I'm sure in His humanity, this could have caused some potential insecurity for Jesus. Have you ever thought what it must have been like for Jesus to be God Himself living in human form? At some point in His childhood He must have begun to recognize that He was different from all the other kids. He was entertaining thoughts such as "I am God. All the fullness of Deity dwells in Me in bodily form." This must have been very peculiar for Him. He must have thought, "Either I am really crazy, or these thoughts are true." With whom could He counsel? Who could understand? Can you imagine going to the Rabbi, "Excuse me, Rabbi, but I have been thinking some very strange thoughts recently. I have had the thoughts that I actually am God, Himself. What do you think about this?"

Perhaps His mother was the only person who could really understand what life might have been like for Jesus. I believe that in His humanity, Jesus experienced the same type of insecurities and fears that we do. If there was any insecurity, unsettledness or doubts left about His identity or destiny, I believe that these things were absolutely set to rest at the Jordan River when The Father pronounced publicly for all to hear, "You are My beloved Son. In You I am well pleased." I believe that this blessing from His heavenly Father gave Jesus the confidence and strength to walk in His true identity in ministry and fulfill His destiny on Earth. God intended for this same type of blessing to come to each one of us from Him through our earthly fathers.

Bar Barakah

Chapter 3
WHO SHOULD BLESS AND WHEN?

You may wonder why I keep referring to the father's blessing at the time of puberty. What about the mother? The mother is also an important role player, but she is not the key role player at the time of puberty. God designed men and women with entirely different roles in the lives of their children. Ungodly people would like us to believe that there is no difference in the role of a mother and father in the life of a child. This is simply not the case. At the time of puberty, the father (not the mother) inherently has the voice of God or Satan to bless or curse his son's or daughter's manhood or womanhood.

A mother was designed by God to fulfill two main functions: 1) **Birth**; and 2) **Nurture** her children. Men were not designed to fulfill these two functions. Despite the movies you might see, men will never give birth to children. Women were physically and emotionally designed by God to fulfill these two functions. I believe that from birth up to the time of puberty the mother is the key role player in the impartation of identity and destiny in love and security in the lives of her children. She is then to turn the children primarily over to the father at the time of puberty.

The father is then designed by God to also fulfill two main functions: **1) Confirm gender identity**; and 2) **Release in destiny**. Even in conception, it is the seed of the father that determines the gender of the child.

Genetically, a girl is determined by two X chromosomes, while a boy is determined by an X and a Y chromosome. Since the mother has two X chromosomes, she is only capable of contributing an X chromosome to the conception, while the father can contribute either an X or a Y, thus determining the gender of the child. God designed the father to determine and confirm gender identity.

Fathers tend to focus their children outward, while mothers tend to focus their children inward. If you have recently noticed the difference in how fathers and mothers hold little children in public, you will have seen this difference in focus manifested. Most mothers hold their babies inward toward themselves in a nurturing sort of way. Most fathers hold their babies on the palm of their hand outward showing the child the world and the world the child. Obviously, children need both parents. In teenage years, the father says, "Send him on a short-term mission trip half way around the world at age 13." The mother says, "No, that's my baby. He'll get hurt." Again, we need both parents in our lives growing up.

So, at the time of puberty the child needs the blessing of the father to confirm gender identity and to be released into adult destiny. This is why the devil fights so hard to remove the father from the lives of the children at the time of puberty. Several years ago I was surprised as I read a study done on divorce in the United States relative to the age of children. The results of this study were graphed as a "bell curve," as are characteristic of many sociological statistics. However, it was very interesting to note that the peak of the bell was at age

12-13 of the first-born child, right at the age of the puberty transition. In other words, more couples in the United States get divorced right as their first-born child approaches age 12 to 13 than at any other time.

If this isn't a scheme of the devil, then I don't know what is. Satan is intent on nullifying the effectiveness of the father in the lives of his children particularly at this critical age. Of course, divorce is not his only tactic. Satan will take the father effectively out of the children's' lives through divorce, death, desertion, apathy, emotional insecurity and unavailability, busyness, or ignorance. When the father is unavailable to impart into the lives of his children God's blessing of identity and destiny, then the children will go in search of it elsewhere. Satan is always happy to oblige them by sending them various surrogate "fathers" and role models who will impart a counterfeit "blessing" and release into adulthood.

I believe that this is why God speaks through the prophet Malachi about turning the hearts of the fathers to their children and the hearts of the children to their fathers.

"Behold, I will send you Elijah the prophet before the coming of the great and dreadful day of the Lord. And he will turn the hearts of the fathers to the children and the hearts of the children to their fathers, lest I come and strike the earth with a curse." **Malachi 4:5-6**

There is usually little problem with the hearts of the mothers being turned toward their children. The problem primarily lies with the fathers. Our prisons and drug rehabilitation centers are full of fatherless sons and daughters. I remember hearing several years ago about a free giveaway program a greeting card company did with Mother's Day cards in a state penitentiary. They offered free cards to anyone who would like one, and were quickly left with a long line of prisoners they had to turn away when the stock ran out. Since this program was so successful, the company decided a few weeks later to make the same offer in the same prison for Father's Day cards. This time they brought three times as many cards so as to be sure not to run out. Much to their surprise, only three cards total were taken. It turned out that each of the prisoners in that facility except three either had no viable relationship with a father, or hated the father they had known.

WHY SOME FATHERS DON'T RELEASE BLESSING TO THEIR CHILDREN

There are three main reasons that I have run into as to why some fathers don't bless their children at the time of puberty and release them into adulthood. **The first reason** is very simple—**ignorance**. Fathers have not been taught, nor did they understand the necessity of blessing in the lives of their children. Their own fathers did not do this for them, so they have not known the need to do this for their own children.

A second reason some fathers won't bless their

children is due to their **lack of understanding the need to separate identity from behavior in the lives of their children**. When identity and behavior are fused in the mind of the father, then he will believe the **lie** that to bless the identity of his child is to condone the behavior of the child. Conversely, in an attempt to discipline the behavior of his child, he will concurrently curse the identity of the child. Is it right to bless a rebellious, misbehaving child? Certainly! A primary root of teenage rebellion is lack of parental blessing. We are meant to bless the person and discipline the behavior. One father remarked in response to this question, "I'll bless him all right: with a two-by-four upside the head."

Thank God that He is able to separate our behavior from our identity. *"But God demonstrates His own love toward us, in that while we were yet sinners, Christ died for us."* Romans 5:8. I can't think of a much greater blessing and confirmation of love than to die for another person. Because Jesus died for you and conveyed His approval and acceptance of you while you were still a rebel against Him, does this mean that He also accepted and approved of your sinful behavior? Of course not! He separated who you are (identity) from what you do (behavior).

CONTROL VS. AUTHORITY

When fathers fail to separate identity from behavior, they fall into the trap of either condoning wrong behavior in an attempt to bless the child, or condemning the child in an attempt to discipline the behavior. When this happens, a father will tend to govern his family using the devil's system of government, rather than God's. God and Satan govern people through two entirely different systems of government. I have come to call Satan's system of governing the system of "**control**." God, on the other hand, governs through the "**exercise of authority**."

Let me define these terms as I will use them here. **Control is: using the manipulative power of the soul to force (threaten or intimidate) others to do your will. The exercise of authority is: honoring the personhood and free-will choice of others by offering them choices with consequences.** Control does not honor or many times even acknowledge the free-will choice of others. The exercise of authority consistently honors the choices of others, but also consistently applies consequences to wrong choices.

God has always honored the choices of people. He has never forced anyone to receive Jesus Christ. He offers choices with consequences. He may say for example, "Choice A: to receive Jesus Christ will result in being in My presence and eternal life in Heaven. Choice B: to reject Jesus Christ in your life will result in separation from Me and eternal death in hell. I highly recommend choice A. It will be much better for you. However, the choice is yours."

In Deuteronomy 30:19 God said, *"I call heaven and earth as witnesses today against you that I have set before you life and death, blessing and cursing; therefore choose life, that you and your descendants may live."*

Again, God is offering choices with consequences. I believe that it was His intention for us to govern our children in that same way in which He governs us. Unfortunately, all some fathers have ever known is control. They were controlled by their parents and have continued using the same methods with their children.

Let me illustrate this point just a little further. Bill grew up under a system of control with his parents. Consequently, when he married and had children of his own, he governed his children the only way he knew, through control. This resulted in tremendous rebellion in and a very strained relationship with his oldest son, Bob, later in teenage years. One night when Bob was seventeen, he locked the door of his room and turned up quite loud a CD playing a type of music his father had forbidden to even be in the house. Bill, the father, came upstairs to his son's room to tell him to turn off that music. As he approached the room, he discovered that not only had his son's rebellion manifested in loud forbidden music, but he also discovered smoke billowing out from under the door. Bill was pretty certain that this was not ordinary tobacco smoke but that it was, instead, Marijuana smoke. Incensed, Bill knocked at the door, ordering Bob to let him in. There was no response. Bill began to pound on the door, shouting at the top of his lungs, demanding his son to open the door this minute. The music only got louder. Furious, Bill stormed back downstairs not knowing what to do.

The next morning when Bob came down for breakfast, there was his dad waiting for him at the table.

Bill verbally tore into Bob, telling him what a worthless human being he was, and expressing sheer hatred through his eyes and voice intonation. Bob endured the tongue-lashing while eating his breakfast, further hardened his heart against his dad, and left for school without uttering one word in response.

If one would have suggested to Bill at this point that he should conduct a ceremony to bless his son and release him into manhood, he would not have been able to do so because of the offense, hurt, frustration, and hatred in his heart toward his son. Not long after this incident, a friend of Bill's shared with him the concept of separating identity from behavior and governing his household through the exercise of authority rather than control. As Bill meditated on what his friend had said to him, the Lord really smote his heart regarding the years of cursing his son's identity in an attempt to control his behavior. Bill wept bitterly before the Lord and determined to change his way of relating to Bob.

The next day, Bill took his son aside and apologized to him for his anger, condemnation, and lack of honor of Bob's right to make a choice. He then explained to Bob the concept of governing through the exercise of authority rather than control. He told him that from now on he would offer Bob choices with consequences, rather than try to force his will on Bob. Bill told his son, "For example, Bob, regarding this matter of locking yourself in your room and not responding to your mother or me, I want to explain to you about two choices you have. When your mother or I come to knock on the door, you could choose Choice A or Choice B. Choice A would be to open the door and discus with us whatever matter is at hand. The consequence of this choice is that you will continue to enjoy the same privilege regarding your room as you now do. On the other hand, you could choose choice B, which is to leave the door locked and not respond to your mother or me. The consequence of this choice is that you will loose some of the privilege you now enjoy regarding your room. I highly recommend choice A. I believe it is a much better choice. Bob, do you understand your choices?" "Yeah, Yeah. Whatever," Bob muttered.

Of course, the next evening Bob decided to test out the new system. He went into his room, turned up the music and smoked his smoke. Bill went upstairs and knocked on his son's door. There was no response. "Oh, I guess he's chosen Choice B," Bill thought to himself. "Oh well, I'll check one more time just to make sure." Bill knocked on the door again and called Bob's name. The music got louder. "Yep, he's chosen Choice B," Bill thought, as he returned back down stairs to continue reading the book in which he had become engrossed.

The next morning, as Bob come down for breakfast, he was shocked to be greeted pleasantly by his father. Bill continued in pleasant conversation asking Bob about the day he had planned. "What have you got going at school today, Bob." Bob told him about various classes and activities for the day. He mentioned that he would be home at about 6:00 pm after soccer practice. His father then remarked, "God sure has gifted you at soccer,

Bar Barakah

Bob. I wouldn't be surprised if you earn a full scholar-
ship to university in soccer. Well, God bless you! Have
a wonderful day." Bob walked out of the house totally
shocked. "What had happened to Dad?" he mused. Maybe
he got saved." (Bill, of course had been a "Christian" for
many years.)

About 6:00 PM that evening when Bob arrived
home, his dad cheerfully greeted him from the living
room as he passed him on his way up to his bedroom.
About 15 seconds later, Bob came running back down to
the living room exclaiming, "Dad, Dad, there's no door
on my room." "I know," remarked Bill. "I was explain-
ing to you about that day before yesterday. Remember?
Choice A and Choice B. Last night you chose B. I had
explained to you that if you preferred Choice B, then
you would lose some privilege regarding your room.
Apparently, you thought that having a door on your room
was a right, but in actuality it was a privilege. You have
lost that privilege for the next couple of weeks. So, if
your mother or I have an issue we need to discuss with
you, we will be able to do so as needed. I personally
would have thought that Choice A would have been a
better choice. If you remember, I did recommend Choice
A. However, you chose B, and that's fine too. God bless
you son. Have a nice evening."

This was the first of many experiences that proved
to rebuild relationship between this father and son. The
father learned how to separate identity from behavior so
that he could love, accept and bless his son at the same
time he disciplined his behavior. Many fathers are unable

to bless their children at the time of puberty, because they have destroyed relationship with them through governing by Satan's system of control. At the time of puberty, the child is already alienated in his/her heart from the father, and the father is offended, hurt, angry and not able to bless and release. Because of negative behavior, he feels compelled to continue to force and control.

A third reason that some fathers are unable to bless their children at the time of puberty is that **they have never received that blessing themselves** and thus have an inability to give that which they have not received. I recently heard a story of just such a situation. A pastor had reached a young woman with the gospel and she gave her life to Christ. This young woman, about age 26, had been involved in great immorality and promiscuity for about the last ten years. As the pastor then began to counsel with her, he said, "Let's pray and ask the Lord what the root of all the immorality in your life is." She responded, "Pastor, we don't even need to pray. I know exactly when and how it started." "You do," he exclaimed. "Tell me about it."

"It started shortly after my sixteenth birthday," she said. "I grew up in a pastor's home, and my parents were quite strict. We were not allowed to go out on dates until we were sixteen. All my friends could date at fourteen, so I thought that this was really unfair. However, finally my sixteenth birthday came and a young man did invite me out on a date. I was so excited because this would be my first date. I was also quite apprehensive, wondering whether he would like me, and if I were really a woman."

"The day of the date finally arrived. I spent several hours getting ready. I wanted to look just right. About a half hour before the young man was to pick me up, I came downstairs into the living room where my father was reading the newspaper. I just needed some kind of affirmation from him that I looked OK and that I really was a woman and not a foolish little schoolgirl. I came into the room and asked him, 'Daddy, how do I look?' Without even looking up from the newspaper, he muttered something unintelligible. I tried again, moving to the side so he could see me from around the paper. He moved the paper to block eye contact. I asked, 'Dad, do I look all right?' 'Yeah, fine,' he said. 'Dad, do you think he'll like me?' Again, he muttered something unintelligible from behind the newspaper. 'Dad, do you want to meet him?' I queried. 'No, you go on,' he replied."

"Shortly after that, the doorbell rang and I left with the young man. Pastor," she said, "I know that as a young woman, I desperately needed my father's love and approval that night to bring security to the haunting question, 'Was I a real woman?' When he wouldn't give it, I shut him out of my life and went looking for the affirmation of my womanhood from other men. When I closed the door to my house that night as I left on the date, I also closed the door of my heart to my father. I said in my heart, 'If he won't pay any attention to me, then I don't need him, and I won't pay any attention to him.'"

The pastor then asked the young woman, "I know your father. He and I have been in ministers' fellowships together for years. Would you mind if I called him and asked him to meet with the two of us?" "I'd like that very much," said the young woman. The pastor then called the father and requested a meeting together with his daughter. The father was overjoyed, and said, "We've been praying for her for over ten years. Yes, I'd love to meet with you."

On the day of the meeting, the pastor asked the young woman to share with her father the things that she had shared with him earlier. She began "Dad, you may not even remember this evening, but it was very important to me. It was the night of my first date. I came down into the living room and you were reading the paper." The father stopped her there and began to fill in the details himself. The pastor, shocked, asked the father, " If you remember that evening in so much detail, why didn't you give your daughter the blessing she was so desperately looking for?"

Tears then began to stream down the father's cheeks. Turning to his daughter, he began to share with her, "Honey, it wasn't because I didn't love you, or didn't know what you were after that evening that I didn't give you what you needed. You see, I never received from my father any affirmation of my manhood. As a result, I found myself that evening a frightened little boy required to do something which only a man could do. When you came downstairs, I didn't know how to relate to you. It seemed like only yesterday that we rocked you in a cradle. How could you have grown up so quickly. I knew how to relate to you as a little girl, but I was scared to death to suddenly find myself relating to a sixteen-year-old woman. I didn't want you to see the scared little boy looking out through my eyes, so I just hid behind the newspaper and prayed for the moment to pass quickly. I felt so inadequate and insecure as a father that I didn't want you to see what was going on inside me. Honey, I'm so sorry that I didn't give you what you so desperately required that evening. Could you please find it in your heart to forgive me?"

The daughter burst into tears and fell into her fathers arms and cried, "Oh Daddy, I didn't know. I thought it was because you didn't care about me." By this time all three of them were in tears and God worked a tremendous reconciliation in that family that day.

WHEN SHOULD THE BLESSING CEREMONY BE CONDUCTED?

In the Jewish culture, the Bar Mitzvah ceremony usually takes place at age thirteen. I believe that the right time for the Bar Barakah ceremony is as the child is coming into puberty. (As is frequently done with the Jewish phrase Bar Mitzvah, I will primarily use only the male form Bar Barakah as a generic term to signify usage either for a man or woman.) This will be somewhat different for different people. In general, it will be between age 12 and 15. This depends upon the emotional maturity of the son or daughter. For example, my children are just approaching this age now. I have delayed this ceremony in the life of my older son, because I can see that he has not been ready. The right time for him will be a little while after his fifteenth birthday. On the other hand, my younger son will be ready right at age thirteen.

It is the job of parents to observe their own children and determine when is the right time. You can tell it is right when the child begins to take an interest in the opposite sex, is thinking about more long-term goals and loses interest in childish pursuits of the past. Just realize that there is no set age, but rather that it will be different for each child.

WHAT ABOUT SINGLE MOMS AND STEP-PARENTS?

You may be asking at this point, "Well, what about single moms? Who can bless and release her children?" This, unfortunately, is one of the tragedies of divorce in our culture. Many times the legitimate authority ordained by God to speak into the lives of his children, namely the father, is unavailable. If he is truly unwilling or unavailable to be involved in the lives of his children in this way, then it is the job of the pastors and elders of the church to minister to the "widows" and "orphans." This is where the godly men of the church need to come alongside such a family and help impart to the children what the father is unavailable to impart. Many times God will also use other key family members, such as a grandfather or an uncle. If you are a single mom, seek the Lord as to whom He would want to use in the lives of your children to impart this blessing at the time of puberty, and wait on the Lord to see whom He is raising up in relationship. You would not want someone fulfilling this role out of a sense of religious duty rather than out of a desire in the heart to bless. As you seek God, He will put the desire to bless in the hearts of the appropriate relatives and Christian leaders.

Another question which I am frequently asked is: Can a step-father bless his stepchildren? The answer is: Yes, especially if the biological father is unavailable, a stepfather has a responsibility to bless his stepchildren. This may well be a key to tearing down any remaining walls of division or estrangement between the stepfather and the son or daughter.

Chapter 4
THREE KEY COMPONENTS TO RELEASE A BAR/BAT BARAKAH (SON/DAUGHTER OF THE BLESSING)

Let me at this point briefly summarize what we have concluded so far. It is God's intent that every son and daughter receive a powerful impartation of identity and destiny from God coming through a father at the time of puberty. This impartation is to come in the form of a public, ceremonial blessing. This blessing empowers the son or daughter to prosper in adulthood. It brings emotional closure to childhood and releases the son or daughter into adulthood. It is so important that Jesus, Himself, did not begin His ministry without first receiving it from His Heavenly Father. This blessing should be imparted by the father and/or other key men in the community of believers. We will suggest that such a released son or daughter be called a Bar/Bat Barakah, a son/daughter of the blessing.

Let's now turn our attention to three critical components necessary to release a son as a Bar Barakah, or a daughter as a Bat Barakah: 1) Instruction, 2) Ceremony, 3) Celebration.

INSTRUCTION

The instruction preceding the ceremony is as important as the ceremony, itself. Unfortunately, because many of us did not receive this type of instruction from our parents, to do so is completely new to us. The first step in the process is to consult your pastor, as you would regarding the marriage of your child. There is included below in this book a list of resource materials listed in this book designed to teach you how to give this instruction to your children. Many people have simply abdicated their responsibility in this area and have hoped that the youth pastor, senior pastor or some other church or school official would provide this instruction. However, the youth pastor will not stand before God to give an account for the instruction given to your children. You, their parents will. Within the church, it is the job of the pastors to equip the parents to impart into their children's lives, not to do it for them. In many churches, pastors have been teaching only the youth, rather than teaching the parents to instruct and impart into the lives of their children.

I believe that this instruction is to be initiated and overseen by the father, but conducted by both father and mother. There is a beautiful window of opportunity which God created in the lives of children for this instruction to take place in just the year or two preceding the onset of adolescence. At around age eleven or twelve, most children are uniquely prepared by God to receive instruction regarding adulthood from their parents. Children's hearts still tend to be very open to their parents at this time in life as they are not yet consumed with as many activities as they will be in a couple of years. Most children still enjoy spending time with their parents at this age.

I believe that the best format in which this instruction might take place is a regular weekly meeting with your son or daughter over a six to twelve month period. During these times, various topics of manhood and womanhood may be discussed. The goal of these times together should be focused far more on relationship and mentorship than on content impartation. Through the course of this instruction, your child is being prepared to take spiritual responsibility for his/her own life from the time of the ceremony onward. Up until that time, the parents carry spiritual responsibility for the spiritual feeding and well-being of the child, but this responsibility is then released to the child at the Bar/Bat Barakah ceremony.

In preparation for instructing your sons and daughters to become Bar/Bat Barakah, I have found some materials that are extremely helpful in structuring your thinking. Firstly, in order to more fully understand the impact of blessing or the lack thereof in the lives of your children, not only at the time of puberty, but also at other key times, I would highly recommend that you that you attend a **Family Foundations Basic Seminar.** In this seminar we identify seven critical times when God intended for parents to bless their children. We also, in this seminar, help parents to receive from God the blessing that they may not have received from their own parents. This enables parents to then give this same blessing to their children. It is very difficult to give to others that which you have not yet received yourself. If you have not yet done so, I would strongly encourage you to attend this seminar in the near future. You can find more information about the Basic Seminar on pages 66-67 in the back of this book

In addition to the seminar, the following books I consider "non-optional" for every parent to read in advance of their children entering into teenage years. This information has not come to us through modeling by our parents, and thus must be relearned. If you would consult with your pastor and read just one of these books each month beginning seven months in advance of the time you wish to begin the instruction with your child, I believe that God would give you the wisdom and confidence to mightily prepare your children for adulthood. Following is a list of the books and tapes:

1) *The Ancient Paths,* by Craig Hill, (Littleton: Family Foundations Publishing, 1992)

2) *Raising Godly Children*, by Craig Hill, (3 cassette series) (Littleton: Family Foundations Publishing, 1993)

3) *The Blessing*, by Gary Smalley and John Trent, Ph.D., (Nashville: Thomas Nelson, Inc., 1986)

4) *Stepping Into Adulthood*, by Jeff Brodsky (Phoenix: ACW Press, 1997)

5) *Raising A Modern Day Knight*, by Robert Lewis, (Colorado Springs: Focus On the Family Publishing, 1997)

6) *Imparting the Blessing to Your Children*, by William T. Ligon, (Workbook and 4 cassette series) (Brunswick: Shalom, Inc. P.O. Box 1218, Brunswick, GA 31521, 1989)

7) *Raising Them Chaste*, by Richard C. Durfield, PH.D. and Renee Durfield, (Minneapolis: Bethany House Publishers, 1991)

You may purchase these materials separately from your local bookstore, or for your convenience, we have put together a "Bar Barakah Parents' Packet #1" combining all these materials which you may purchase from the nearest Family Foundations International office. For a listing of these offices see page 68 in the back of this book.

Let's talk now about the actual instruction time between parents and their son or daughter. **This instruction time is meant to prepare the child for the following five things**.

1) To enter into a settled sense of adult identity.

2) To enter into a clear, settled sense of destiny and purpose including a personal mission statement.

3) To be emotionally released into manhood or womanhood at the time of the Bar/Bat Barakah ceremony.

4) To take adult responsibility for his/her own spiritual health from the time of the ceremony on.

5) To walk in emotional and sexual purity all the days of his/her life.

One of the most powerful tools I have found to help in this preparation process is the **Institute In Basic Life Principles Seminar** (IBLP) conducted by Mr. Bill Gothard. This seminar is conducted over four evenings and two full days and entails thirty-two hours of teaching, diagrams and charts. Basic principles of life which everyone needs to know, and most people don't, are clearly brought to light through this seminar. Topics include the following:

- Resolving family conflict
- Developing godly character in your life
- Accepting God's unchangeable design for your life
- Accepting responsibility and responding correctly to authority
- Responding correctly to injustice
- Gaining and keeping a clear conscience
- Conquering worry and anger through yielding your personal rights to God
- Walking in moral purity and freedom
- Discovering purpose and true success in life
- Learning God's wisdom in building genuine friendships
- Relating properly as a single person to people of the opposite sex
- Discerning God's will in choosing a marriage partner

I believe that the principles taught in this seminar are basic preparation for life. It would behoove every father to make this seminar a mandatory part of the preparation process for Bar Barakah for each of his sons and daughters. I would suggest that you set aside a special week, if at all possible, just to spend with your son/daughter and attend this seminar together. You may use time outside the seminar structure to cover other Bar Barakah topics, and to have some fun time together. This IBLP seminar will provide topics and material which you can continue to discuss with your son/daughter for many months following. I first attended an ILBP seminar when I was twenty years old, and I would say that through the years, the material taught in this seminar has had a more profound, long-lasting effect on my life than any I have ever encountered elsewhere. I can't encourage you enough to attend this seminar with each of your children in preparation for their Bar/Bat Barakah ceremony. For a schedule of future seminars in your area, you may write: Institute in Basic Life Principles, Box One, Oak Brook, IL 60522-3001 USA, Telephone: (708) 323-9800. If this seminar has not yet come to the nation in which you live, you may want to contact the Institute in Basic Life Principle to discover what would be necessary to bring the seminar to your country.

In addition to the above-mentioned seminar, I believe a father needs to cover at least the following topics with his children. Many of these topics are covered in detail in the IBLP seminar, but may be discussed and worked into the child's life in mentoring relationship with his/her parents. Each church and each family may want to emphasize somewhat different points, and thus personalize the instruction to fit your specific family and fellowship. Below is at least a start on some topics that I believe are essential.

1) What is a man/woman?
    A. God's model of three-part being.
    B. Spiritual responsibilities and relationship with God.
    C. Character qualities of a godly man/woman.
    D. Man/woman as a sexual being.
    E. Responsibility to work.

2) Relationship with members of the opposite sex.
   A. How to treat a woman/man.
   B. Courtship vs. dating. Protection of the heart by the father.
   C. Discerning God's will in marriage partner selection.
   D. How to deal with sexual attraction and avoid lust.
3) Wisdom in making choices.
   A. Long-term effect and generational consequences of choices made in teenage years.
4) Financial management and accountability.
   A. Provision
   B. Tithing
   C. Giving
   D. Saving
   E. Lending
   F. Spending
   G. Avoidance of debt.
5) Vision and faith. God's purpose and destiny in life.
   A. Develop together a personal life-mission statement.
   B. Review scriptures and prophetic words given over your son/daughter.
   C. Living a life of service to God and others vs. a life of self-service.
   D. Make plans to participate on a short-term missions outreach team.
6) Wisdom in choosing right friendships and associations.

7) Your unique family heritage and destiny.

Let me list for you here some materials that I believe should be studied by both the child and the parents. These materials should be read or listened to together and then discussed and applied to your specific situation. Again, because these things were not taught us by our parents, many of these OLAM Ancient Ways of God are not familiar to us, and we must now learn them ourselves in order to instruct our children. Therefore, these materials are essential in preparing your son or daughter for making some of the commitments he/she may choose to make at his/her Bar/Bat Barakah ceremony.

1) *His Perfect Faithfulness*, by Eric and Leslie Ludy (Littleton: Family Foundations Publishing, 1996)
2) *Romance God's Way*, by Eric and Leslie Ludy (Longmont: Makarios Publishing, 1997)
3) *Walking With the Wise*, by Benny and Sherree Phillips (Gaithersburg: People of Destiny, 1994)
4) *Biblical Standards of Courtship*, by Jonathan Lindvall (Oak Brook: Institute in Basic Life Principles, 1993)
5) *Relationships*, by Dean Sherman (Four video tape series) (YWAM Publishing, 1996)
6) *God's Principles of Finance*, by Craig Hill (Audio tape series) (Family Foundations Publishing, 1996)

Again, you may choose to purchase these materials separately, or for your convenience we have put together a "Bar Barakah Packet #2" combining all these materials which you may purchase from the nearest Family Foundations International office. For a listing of these offices see page 68 in the back of this book.

I was shocked recently when I heard a speaker make the statement that one hundred years ago in North America ninety percent of the people worked for themselves, and ten percent of the population were employed by others. "Today," however, he continued, "these statistics are reversed. Only ten percent of the population work for themselves, and ninety percent work for others." One hundred years ago most people were engaged in fulfilling a calling or dream in their hearts. Most people loved their work and pursued it, because they considered it a part of their purpose and destiny in life. Today, many people hate their job, have no vision, and work only fulfilling someone else's vision in order to financially survive. **One hundred years ago parents prepared their children to discover a calling and fulfill a destiny. Today, most parents set their sights no higher than to prepare their children to find a "good paying job."**

Over the last hundred years, dream killers have entered into our society and robbed many people of their God-given dreams and destiny. Most of our education system is geared to teach people how to get a job, not how to discover a purpose and fulfill a destiny. One of the most powerful paradigm shifts you can help your child make is that God did not create him/her to simply have a job. He created your child with unique giftings and anointing to fulfill a purpose which no one else can fulfill. It is your duty as a parent to seek the Lord regarding your children's destinies and continually work at imparting to them and preparing them to fulfill their destinies. This discussion of your child's destiny should play a significant role in the Bar Barakah instruction time.

Another critical role of parents is to provide their children with age-appropriate sexual information. This should happen throughout their growing-up years, not just at one time. I believe that it is God's intention for a father to be the primary source of sexual information to both his son and daughter. They are not meant to learn sexual misinformation from peers, other adults, magazines, or movies. While it is important that both parents participate in the sexual education of their children, it is especially important in this Bar Barakah preparation time that the father has several open discussions on this topic with both his son and his daughter. Many fathers, out of their own insecurity and embarrassment, delegate any discussions of anatomy, sexuality, puberty, and menstruation with their daughters to the mother. This is not healthy. I have found that the way a father relates to his daughter at this critical time in life prepares her spiritually and emotionally for relationship with her husband. If her father shuns her sexuality and femininity as shameful or embarrassing, the daughter will tend to expect the same from her future husband as well. This is why it is very important for a father to be involved along with his wife in discussions with his daughter about her own growing sexuality.

It would be well for a father to share with his son

as he approaches puberty something like the following: "Son, in the next few months to a year you will notice many changes coming to pass in your life. You will notice physical, emotional and intellectual changes. You will find yourself thinking some thoughts that you have never thought before. You will find yourself feeling some feelings that you have never felt before. You will begin to grow hair on parts of your body where you have never had hair before."

"Son, in the next little while, your physical appearance will become very important to you. You will begin to care deeply how you look to other people, especially girls. You will also begin to experience thoughts of sexual attraction toward girls. I know that right now this may not make any sense to you, but I want you to remember what I'm telling you for the future. You will find yourself wanting to spend time with girls and you will feel feelings of sexual attraction towards them. Son, I want you to know that these changes are of God, not the devil. God is the One Who made us sexual beings. Sexual attraction, in and of itself, is not dirty or unclean. It is good and right and pure. God created you to be sexually attracted to women. But, son, there is a difference between sexual attraction and lust. If you do not learn how to properly handle sexual thoughts they will develop into lust, which is not of God and will destroy your life. I know what I am talking about, son, because I have had to deal with these same thoughts and feelings myself. I want to teach you how to talk to Jesus Christ and to release these thoughts and feelings to Him. Son, when you begin to have such thoughts and feelings, I want you to start talking to me about these things, because I can help you to properly handle them, OK? I want to walk with you through this time in your life."

A father should also be able to speak to his daughter in a similar way. "Honey, you are growing up, and in the next few months to a year you will experience many things changing in your life. You will begin to think some thoughts that you have never thought before and feel some feelings that you have never felt before. You will begin to have thoughts and feelings of sexual attraction toward boys. This is not wrong or evil. It is natural and designed by God. Sexual relationship is not something dirty, unclean, or impure. However, if you do not learn how to release your sexual thoughts and emotions to Jesus, Satan will try to develop this God-given attraction gift into lust. Lust is impure and is very destructive."

"You will find many young men who want to relate to you on a sexual basis in lust. You may feel like you have to protect yourself continually from them. However, God never intended for you to have to protect your own heart from the lust of young men. God placed me in your life to be the protector of your emotional and sexual purity. So, if you find a young man flirting with you, or expressing more than a friendship interest in you, please just give him my card and tell him to call and make an appointment with me. I will be happy to meet with him to determine if he is sent from God as a potential marriage partner for you." (Obviously, prior to this discussion, you should have already covered with your daughter the materials by Eric and Leslie Ludy and Jonathan Lindvall.)

"Honey, in the next few months to a year, you will also experience many changes in your physical body. You will begin to grow hair in places where you have previously had none. You will also one day find yourself vaginally bleeding. I know that this is sort of embarrassing to talk about, but I want you to know that this is completely normal. When it happens, I don't want you to be scared, or to think that you are dying or are really sick, or that something is terribly wrong with your body. This is normal and was designed by God to happen to every girl as she becomes a woman. This bleeding is part of a normal cycle of life that cleanses your body and will give you the ability to bear children one day. You don't have to be afraid of it or embarrassed about it. When this cycle begins in your body, your mom and I want to celebrate with you, because this will begin to mark your transition from being a little girl into being a woman."

If you will have these type of open discussions with your son and daughter, you will move toward keeping an open relationship with them over the next few years in which you can continue to bless and guide them as they learn to walk in their own adult identity and destiny. Again, this is not meant to be a sample of "the talk" you should have with your children. I believe rather, that as you pursue relationship with your children, you will have opportunities to have many such discussions with them.

CEREMONY

The time of instruction is meant to be culminated in a Bar/Bat Barakah ceremony releasing the son or daughter into adulthood. This ceremony helps to create an emotional closure to childhood and a release into adulthood. As I mentioned earlier, this ceremony is no small thing, but rather should be granted as much priority and importance as a wedding. There should be as much planning and preparation, as much money spent, and as many people invited to the Bar Barakah ceremony as there would be to your child's wedding. Robert Lewis in his book, *Raising A Modern Day Knight* outlines the following four key components of a significant ceremony.

Lewis states that memorable ceremonies are first of all **costly.**[1] That which costs you nothing conveys little value. When King David wanted to erect an altar to the Lord on the threshing floor of Araunah, the Jebusite, Araunah offered to give his threshing floor to the king. But David responded to Araunah saying, *" 'No, but I will surely buy it from you for a price; nor will I offer burnt offerings to the Lord my God with that which costs me nothing.' So David bought the threshing floor and the oxen for fifty shekels of silver,"* II Samuel 24:24. David understood that the expenditure of money conveys value. I'm not suggesting that you must spend tens of thousands of dollars on your child's Bar Barakah ceremony, but I do believe that the expenditure should parallel that of a wedding.

Lewis states secondly that a significant ceremony

ascribes value to the individual.[2] By "making a big deal" out of the Bar Barakah ceremony you are making a statement to your child, "You are important. This moment is important."

The third key component of a memorable ceremony which Lewis outlines is that it should **employ meaningful symbols.**[3] There should be a tangible token which your child will keep as a remembrance of the Bar Barakah day. This may be a ring or locket, an article of clothing, a certificate, or some other such physical symbol. Primitive tribal peoples would make permanent marks on the physical body as tokens of passing through a meaningful ceremony. I believe that much of the body piercing that takes place today among young people is the devil's counterfeit of the legitimate need for a tangible, visible token of manhood/womanhood.

Fourthly, Lewis talks about a memorable ceremony **empowering the life with vision.**[4] It creates a transition moment. The ceremony conveys in a powerful way the message, "Your life will never be the same again. You are entering into a new season." This happened for Jesus at the Jordan river. It happens for a Jewish son at his Bar Mitzvah ceremony, and it happens for every married couple at the wedding ceremony. We are wanting to convey to our children at their Bar Barakah ceremony the message, "Your life will be totally different from now on. You will never be a little boy/girl again."

Richard and Renee Durfield in their book, *Raising Them Chaste*,[5] introduce the concept of a "Key Talk" with a son or daughter at the time of puberty. This "Key Talk" entails a special dinner with the same-sex parent in which the son or daughter is invited to ask any questions they have about adulthood, sexuality or other such issues. Sexual purity is explained to the child, who is then asked to make a commitment to save his/her virginity for a marriage partner. In symbolic commemoration of this commitment, the son or daughter is then presented with a ring or locket representing sexual virginity. This is to be worn until the wedding day, at which time it is removed and ceremonially presented to the son's or daughter's marriage partner.

I believe that this "Key Talk" is a wonderful idea to pursue with your children shortly in advance of the actual Bar Barakah ceremony. I would suggest using this dinner as a time for your son/daughter to ask any final questions and just to celebrate the completion of this initial time of instruction. You may want to sign a covenant certificate with your child regarding courtship, such as the one provided in Jonathan Lindwell's booklet, "Biblical Standards of Courtship." I would suggest saving the giving of a ring or significant token for the actual Bar Barakah ceremony itself.

Another tradition that has become popular in some congregations is a weekend men's retreat to welcome new Bar Barakahs into the fellowship of men. A similar women's retreat is also held to welcome young women who have recently passed through their Bat Barakah ceremony into the fellowship of women. I believe that such retreats are also very valuable, because we do not pursue the journey into manhood or womanhood in isolation, but rather together in community with others.

Let us now turn our attention to the actual format of the Bar/Bat Barakah ceremony, itself. Of course, in your specific family and congregation, you must tailor the ceremony to suit your particular culture and situation. However, I will give you below some generic guidelines of commitments to be made and a suggested format to be followed in the ceremony.

Commitments to be made by the Young Person:

1. To dedicate one's life to serving Jesus the Messiah and from this time forth to take spiritual responsibility for his/her own life.

2. To understand and live in accordance with God's 7 non-optional principles of life as outlined in the Institute of Basic Life Principles seminar.

3. To relate to members of the opposite sex while single in accordance with the principles of godly friendship and courtship as opposed to dating. To make a specific commitment to a lifetime of:

    A Sexual purity,

    B. Emotional purity, and

    C. Marital fidelity in covenant.

4. To a life mission statement as understood at this age.

5. To an ongoing relationship with parents, and to a continued honor of them as God's primary instruments of character growth and development.

6. To proper stewardship of wealth and money.

7. To honor all legitimate authority in life (parental, church, school, civil).

Commitments to be made by Parents:
1. To love their son/daughter.
2. To pray for him/her regularly.
3. To teach him/her God's principles of life.
4. To continue to honor him/her with open communication and understanding.
5. To be available for counsel.
6. To partner in prayer with him/her regarding God's choice and timing of a marriage partner.
7. To continue to apply age-appropriate, godly discipline to his/her life as God directs for character development.

Suggestions for a Bar Barakah ceremony format for a son:
1. Worship
2. Introduction of the ceremony by the pastor
3. Pastor's charge to adulthood
4. Special music
5. Message by the pastor
6. Son recites his commitments
7. Parents recite their commitments
8. Reading of past prophecies and words given to son
9. His mother prays over him and blesses him. She remains standing with him.
10. The men of the congregation with his father and grandfathers then call him to come forth from his mother to cross some type of transition line (maybe a physical bridge or some sort of line, barrier, or threshold) into manhood and fellowship with the community of men. He leaves his mother and crosses over to be with the men.

11. His father and grandfathers, receive him as a man and pray their blessing over him, giving him scriptures and prophetic words as the Lord has directed them.

12. Other significant men in the congregation pray, prophesy and bless the new Bar Barakah (Son of the Blessing).

13. The men receive communion together, sealing his manhood by the blood of Messiah.

14. His father gives him a ring (or other such symbol) to be worn as a token of purity and commitment to his vows of manhood until the day of his wedding.

15. Pastor makes final declaration of manhood, prays closing prayer, and all are dismissed to the celebration.

Suggestions for a Bat Barakah ceremony format for a daughter:

1. Worship
2. Introduction of the ceremony by the pastor
3. Pastor's charge to adulthood
4. Special music
5. Message by the pastor
6. Daughter recites her commitments
7. Parents recite their commitments
8. Reading of past prophecies and words given to daughter
9. Both parents pray over her and release her to be a woman. They then leave her where she is standing. (The father then sits down in the congregation. The mother joins the other women.)
10. The women of the congregation with her mother and grandmothers then call her to come out of girlhood and

to cross some type of transition line (maybe a physical bridge or some sort of line, barrier, or threshold) into womanhood and fellowship with the community of women.

11. Her mother and grandmother receive her as a woman and pray their blessing over her, giving her scriptures and prophetic words as the Lord has directed them.

12. Other significant men and women in the congregation pray, prophesy and bless the new Bat Barakah (Daughter of the Blessing).

13. The women receive communion together, sealing her womanhood by the blood of Messiah.

14. Her father prays his blessing over her and gives her a ring (or other such symbol) to be worn as a token of purity and commitment to her vows of womanhood until the day of her wedding.

15. Pastor makes final declaration of womanhood, prays closing prayer, and all are dismissed to the celebration.

SAMPLE PRAYER OF
THE FATHER'S BLESSING

Many people have asked me for a sample of the father's blessing to be prayed over a child in a Bar Barakah ceremony. Obviously there is no standard prayer that can be embraced, as each parent must pray from the heart those things that the Holy Spirit has led him/her to pray over the child. However, in order to give you some idea of a direction in which to seek the Lord, I have enclosed the following guidelines and sample prayer of blessing.

A sample type of prayer to be prayed over a young person at the Bar Barakah ceremony should include at least the following five components:
1) a confirmation of gender identity,
2) a release into manhood or womanhood,
3) a calling forth of positive character qualities,
4) a recital of any prophetic words which have been given over the son or daughter,
5) a pronouncement of specific personal blessing of the father and mother to the child.

Following is a sample prayer and blessing of a father to his son.

"Father God, I thank you for my son, Bob. Bob, you are no longer a little boy. Today you have become a man. You are well equipped with everything you need to fulfill your destiny as a man of God. Before the foundation of the earth, God Almighty planned for your life and planned for you to be a man. There is nothing that you will ever need to do to become a man, because God has made you one. Today we are simply recognizing publicly what God has done in you."

(Recognize specific character qualities in the son.) "Bob, I have noticed in your life that God has made you very intelligent. He has also given you a gift of articulate speech and an ability to take complicated concepts and make them simple for others to understand. I believe that the Lord will use you powerfully to teach his Word to others. You also have a gift as a peacemaker. I notice that when your friends are at odds with each other, God frequently gives you just the right words to break down the walls of enmity and help them reconcile with each other. I believe that God will use you greatly in these areas of reconciliation and teaching."

"Son, I am so glad that God has given you to our family as a gift. You are a wonderful son. I love you! Today I am so proud of you. I bless you with wisdom from God, with emotional security, with sexual purity and marital fidelity. May God continue to prosper you in all that you do, and may you serve the Lord Jesus Christ all the days of your life. Today, I loose you from being your mother's little boy, and I release to you the authority and responsibility of manhood. Bob, today before God and these witnesses, as your father, I declare that you are a man. I love you, son, and I release you to fulfill your destiny in Christ."

CELEBRATION

No ceremony is complete without a party afterwards to celebrate. This Bar/Bat Barakah celebration could be likened much to a wedding reception. Again, I will make some suggestions here, but you need to design a reception for your child appropriate to your own culture. Most people don't need much instruction in how to have a celebration party.

Firstly, I believe that this reception should be held at the same type of place in which you would hold a wedding reception (church fellowship hall, hotel ballroom, restaurant, back yard of home, etc.). Just as at a wedding reception, you may wish to serve your guests dinner, or just light refreshments. In any case, you will want to have a cake to honor your son/daughter. It is entirely appropriate at such a celebration for the guests to further bless the young man or woman with gifts or money (perhaps toward future education or missions trips). You may also wish to have a praise and worship band present to provide music.

It has been a tradition in the Jewish culture for the men of the community to lift the young man seated on a chair upon their shoulders and dance with him around the reception hall. Often his father would accompany them proclaiming loudly for all to hear, "This is my beloved son, in whom I am well pleased." You may or may not wish to embrace this and other aspects of Jewish tradition, but, in any case, I encourage you to develop your own traditions appropriate to your congregation and culture.

After the guests have eaten and fellowshipped for a while, you may want to then open up the microphone for a time of further verbal blessing of your child by others. Perhaps you, as parents, will want to speak some more informal words of blessing to your child. You may want to invite specific, other important people in your child's life to pray or speak something to him/her. There may be friends who have written poems or songs that they would like to share. This is a time when you may wish to allow any appropriate person to share a scripture, prophetic word, prayer, poem, song, story recounting his/her godly character, etc. with which to bless your son/daughter. It would be important here to clearly state that anything shared is to be of a nature that blesses and edifies. Stories or words that embarrass, belittle or shame would not be appropriate, and would be censored.

FOOTNOTES:
[1]Robert Lewis, *Raising A Modern-Day Knight*, (Colorado Springs: Focus on the Family Publishing, 1997) p. 103
[2]*ibid. p. 103*
[3]*ibid. p. 103*
[4]*ibid. p. 103-104*
[5]Richard C. Durfield, PH.D. and Renee Durfield, *Raising Them Chaste*, (Minneapolis: Bethany House Publishers, 1991), pp. 25-34.

Chapter 5
AFTER THE CEREMONY

SHORT-TERM MISSIONS OUTREACH

After releasing your child into adulthood through a Bar/Bat Barakah ceremony, I believe that one of the best ways you can solidify your child's personal relationship with the Lord is to encourage him/her to go on a short-term mission outreach team with other Christian young people. I have noticed that many kids growing up in Christian families primarily relate to the Lord through their parents. Many times they have not really ever had a need to receive guidance from God directly for themselves and have not developed their personal relationship with the Lord outside of their own family context. Many have never seen anything supernatural happen through their own prayers, and have never felt that God spoke to them personally. They have only heard their parents and church leaders tell such stories.

I believe that young men and women need to have the personal experience of seeing someone supernaturally healed when they laid their hands on them and prayed, not just to hear about it from parents and other older adults. I have several times seen Christian young people grow up on the mission field where miracles are happening daily in the lives of their parents, and yet languish in their own relationship with God due to a lack of personal involvement. Even kids living on the mission field need to be released by their parents to go on a team to another location and get involved in letting God speak to and work through them personally. Contrary to popular belief, the word "**GO**" as stated by Jesus in the "Great Commission" recorded in Matthew 28:19 really does imply **a change of location**.

Many people tend to become very self-focused during teenage years. Participating on a Christian outreach team in another country helps remove this self-focus and redirect your son's or daughter's focus back toward God's heart for others. Participation on such a team also forces him/her to make daily decisions based on receiving personal guidance from the Lord and to develop his/her own ministry.

You may choose to go on a short-term mission team with your son or daughter yourself first, or even take your entire family. This may prove to be a very powerful bonding experience between you and your child, and may whet the appetite of your son or daughter for more such experience with the Lord. However, I would greatly encourage you to subsequently release your son or daughter as a young man or woman in whom you demonstrate trust to go on at least one (hopefully many) short-term Christian outreach team by himself/herself.

One of the ways that you can significantly honor your son or daughter as a man or woman is to convey to him or her that you trust him/her in making wise decisions. Many children feel dishonored all of their lives by parents who refuse to trust God to lead their children in decision making. I was just recently ministering to a fifty-year old woman who felt that even to the present time her parents did not trust her decisions, and in relationship with them, they still made her feel like a foolish little girl. As parents, it is important for us to remember that our children will make many mistakes in their learning process, just as we did, but that we can trust God to lead them and keep them safe from significant harm, as we incrementally release them to make decisions.

God continues to raise up many excellent ministries through which young people can participate in short-term mission teams. You may wish to consult with your pastor as to which ones he would recommend for you to investigate. Two ministries with years of experience and a tremendous track record of having taken tens and hundreds of thousands of Christian young people on short-term outreach teams are:

1) **Youth With A Mission**, (YWAM International, Box 85-A, 7085 Battle Creek Rd., Salem, OR 97301, 503-364-3837; e-mail: ywam@xc.org) and

2) **Teen Mania**, (Teen Mania Ministries, PO Box 2000, Garden Valley, Texas 75771-2050; e-mail: webstuff @teenmania.org)

I highly encourage you to contact YWAM, Teen Mania or a missions organization that your pastor would recommend, and begin to talk to your son or daughter about participating on a short-term mission team soon after you release him/her to be a Bar/Bat Barakah.

CONCLUSION AND CHECKLIST

In conclusion, I want to tell you that it is not nearly as important how you conduct your child's Bar/Bat Barakah training, ceremony, and celebration, but rather that you do so. Can you imagine the impact that the Church could have on society in just one generation by reinstituting this simple (OLAM) Ancient Path back into our Church culture? We would have a generation of young men and women who have a strong sense of identity and destiny, and who are empowered by the Holy Spirit to fulfill a destiny, not to just spend a lifetime as wanderers on the earth. We have in our hands as parents the ability to empower our children to prosper in all respects far beyond our own prosperity through learning how to bless and release them into adulthood.

Let me now in closing provide you with a simple checklist that you can use in preparation for releasing your own son as a Bar Barakah (Son of the Blessing) or daughter as a Bat Barakah (Daughter of the Blessing).

❑ Make an appointment with your pastor to discuss and solicit his counsel and help in the entire process
❑ Purchase Bar Barakah Parents' Packet #1
❑ Pick a proposed date and begin preparing for your child's ceremony (Make sure you leave enough time to read the materials and train your child. If you are starting from scratch, I would suggest that this should be at least 18 months.)

❑ Study all the materials in the Bar Barakah Parents' Packet #1 (This is a minimal investment into the life of your child.)

❑ Purchase Bar Barakah Parents' Packet #2 to go over with your child

❑ Establish and conduct a regular, weekly time of Bar/Bat Barakah training with your child

❑ At least 6 months in advance solidify the date of your child's ceremony

❑ Meet with your pastor to plan the Bar/Bat Barakah ceremony

❑ Book the church or facility in which to conduct your child's ceremony

❑ Book the reception/celebration facility

❑ Book any desired reception catering

❑ Book any desired praise and worship bands

❑ Meet with your child to create a guest list (relatives, your friends, your child's friends, spiritual leaders, teachers, others the Lord leads you to invite)

❑ In agreement with your child, select and print invitations

❑ Send invitations

❑ Select and purchase or make any desired ring or other token to be given to your child

❑ Schedule a "Key Talk" if so desired

❑ Contact Christian missions organizations for information and help your son or daughter make plans to participate in a short-term mission outreach team

You won't want to miss the:
Family Foundations Basic Seminar
(From Curse to Blessing)

What Is It?

An intensive time of teaching from God's Word, followed by sharing, prayer, and ministry in small groups. As teaching topics are brought up, the small groups give opportunity for ministry in that specific area of the individual's life, marriage, or family. The seminar is conducted in a Thursday evening, Friday evening, and all day Saturday format.

Topics include:

Communication
> Recognizing different levels of communication.
> Resolving Conflicts.

Individual and Family Purpose and Plan
> Overview of God's plans and purposes for the individual and family.

Identity and Destiny
> 7 Critical Times of Blessing.

Life Patterns
> 8 Adult Life Patterns.
> Impact of lack of blessing or the cursing of identity.

Curses and Blessing
> Releasing God's Blessing.
> Practical steps to freedom from cursing.
> Personal Ministry.

Vision Of the Family Foundations Basic Seminar

It is our vision and purpose to help reimpart back into the culture of the body of Christ, those safeguards which facilitate the natural impartation to people of identity and destiny from God. Without such, the devil has been allowed to impart his message of worthlessness and purposelessness to millions of people throughout the earth.

Who should come?

Anyone desirous of lasting change in your life. Many times we see unpleasant, or unhealthy patterns in our lives, but don't know why they are there and/or can't seem to change. This ministry is designed to identify root causes and bring lasting changes to these areas.

For a schedule of future seminars or for information on how your church can schedule a *Family Foundations Basic Seminar*, please mail the attached form or call, or fax:

Telephone: (303) 797-1139   Fax: (303) 797-1579

Please send me information about the seminars.

Name _____

Address _____

City, State, Zip _____

Telephone _____

Mail to:

In North America
Family Foundations Int'l.
P.O. Box 320
Littleton, Colorado 80160
(303) 797-1139
e-mail: info@FamilyFI.org

In Europe
Family Foundations Int'l.
P.O. Box 52
Rugeley, Staffs.
WS15 3YZ England

In Australia and the Pacific
Family Foundations Int'l.
4 Prunus Place
Caloundra, Queensland 4551
Australia
e-mail: ffiauste@beachaccess.com.au

In Africa
Family Foundations Int'l.
57 Marlborough Road
Harare, Zimbabwe
e-mail: renewalmin@mango,zw

For a current catalog of books and tapes by Craig Hill and
other Family Foundations authors and speakers,
Please write:

In North America
Family Foundations International
P.O. Box 320
Littleton, Colorado 80160
(303) 797-1139
web site: info@FamilyFI.org

In Europe
Family Foundations International
P.O. Box 52
Rugeley, Staffs.
WS15 3YZ England

In Australia and the Pacific
Family Foundations International
4 Prunus Place
Caloundra, Queensland 4551
e-mail: ffiaust@beachaccess.com.au

In Africa
Family Foundations International
57 Marlborough Road
Harare, Zimbabwe
e-mail: renewalmin@mango.zw